Python Data Scie

The Ultimate Crash Course, Tips, and Tricks to

Learn Data Analytics, Machine Learning, and

Their Application

Steve Eddison

Table of Contents

Introduction

Chapter 1: What is Data Science?

The Importance of Data Science

How Is Data Science Used?

The Lifecycle of Data Science

The Components of Data Science

Chapter 2: The Basics of the Python Language

The Statements

The Keywords

Working with Comments

How to Name Your Identifiers

The Importance of Variables

Chapter 3: Why Use Python for Data Science?

Chapter 4: The Best Python Libraries for Data Science, and How They Can Help Get the Job Done

NumPy

SciPy

Pandas

Matplotlib

Scikit-Learn

Theano

TensorFlow

Keras

Chapter 5: The Basics for the Data Life Cycle

Gathering our Data

Preparing the Data

Model Planning

Build the Model

Operationalize

Communicate the Results

Chapter 6: What is Data Mining?

How Does Data Mining Work?

Why Is It So Important?

Data Warehousing and Mining Software

Chapter 7: Some of the Basics of Data Mining with Python

Creating a Regression Model in Python

Chapter 8: Your Complete Course to Working with the Pandas Library

Chapter 9: Using Your Data to Make Smart Business Decisions

Conclusion

Introduction

Congratulations on purchasing *Python Data Science* and thank you for doing so.

The following chapters will discuss everything that we need to know in order to get started with the process of data science and using it for our own needs as well. There is a lot of buzz in the business world, no matter what industry it is, about machine learning, the Python language, and of course, data science, and being able to put these terms together and learn how they work can make a big difference in how well your business will do now and in the future. There are already a ton of companies out there who have been able to gain a competitive edge with data science and the various models and algorithms of Python that go with it, and you can as well.

In this guidebook, we are going to take some time to explore the different parts that come with Python data science. We will start out with some information on what data science is all about and how it can be so beneficial to your business and helping you to gain that competitive edge that you have always wanted. From there, we are going to spend some time exploring the Python language and how this can fit into the world of data science. We will look at some of the basics of the Python coding language, why we should work with Python to help with our data science project and the basic libraries that work with Python and can help us to create some of the models that we need.

After we have an introduction to both Python and data science, it is time to move on to some more of the parts that we need to know in order to work on our own data science project. We are going to explore the basics of the data life cycle to see how this is going to fit into our plan. From gathering the raw data to organizing and cleaning it, to finally being able to analyze the data and learn some of the insights and hidden patterns that we want, this data life cycle is going to be so important to our overall goals.

In addition to learning about the data life cycle and what this means for some of our processes, we need to move on to some of the basics of data mining and how this process works, as well as looking at how we can use the Python coding language to handle some problems of regression, to help us see exactly how data science is going to work for our needs. We can then finish up with a look at the Pandas library, one of the best libraries out there to help us out with machine learning, and a summary of some of the ways that we are able to use all of that data that we have collected, and the steps that we are doing in this process, in order to make some of the best business decisions that we can.

All of this is going to come together in order to strengthen our business and ensure that we are getting the results that we want in every aspect of that business as well. When you are ready to learn more about Python data science and what it is able to do for you and your business, make sure to check out this guidebook to get started.

There are plenty of books on this subject on the market, thanks again for choosing this one! Every effort was made to ensure it is full of as much useful information as possible, please enjoy it!

Chapter 1: What is Data Science?

The first thing that we need to take some time looking over in this guidebook is the basics of data science. Data science, to keep things simple, is the detailed study of the flow of information from the huge amounts of data that a company has gathered and stored. It is going to involve obtaining some meaningful insights out of raw, and usually unstructured, data, that can then be processed through analytical programming and business skills.

Many companies are going to spend a lot of time collecting data and trying to use it to learn more about their customers, figure out how to release the best product, and learning how to gain a competitive edge over others. While these are all great goals, just gathering the data is not going to be enough to make it happen. Instead, we need to be able to take that data, and that data is usually pretty messy and needs some work and analyze it so that we are better able to handle all that comes with it.

The Importance of Data Science

In a world that is going more and more over to the digital space, organizations are going to deal with unheard of amounts of data, but structured and unstructured, on a daily basis. Evolving technologies are going to enable some cost savings for us, and smarter storage spaces to help us store some of this critical data.

Currently, no matter what kind of industry we are looking at or what kind of work the company does, there is already a huge need for skilled and knowledgeable data scientists. They are actually some of the highest-paid IT professionals right now, mainly because they can provide such a good value for the companies they work for, and because there is such a shortage in these professionals. The gap of data scientists versus the current supply is about 50 percent, and it is likely to continue growing as more people and companies start to see what value data science can have for them.

So, why is data becoming so important to these businesses? In reality, data has always been important, but today, because of the growth in the internet and other sources, there is an unprecedented amount of data to work through. In the past, companies were able to manually go through the data they had, and maybe use a few business intelligence tools to learn more about the customer and to make smart decisions. But this is nearly impossible for any company to do now thanks to a large amount of data they have to deal with on a regular basis.

In the last few years, there has been a huge amount of growth in something known as the Internet of Things, due to which about 90 percent of the data has been generated in our current world. This sounds even more impressive when we find out that each day, 2.5 quintillion bytes of data are generated and used, and it is more accelerated with the growth of the IoT. This data is going to come to us from a lot of different sources, and where you decide to gather this data is going to depend on your goals and what you are hoping to accomplish in the process. Some of the places where we are able to gather this kind of data will include:

1. Sensors that are used in malls and other shopping locations in order to gather more information about the people who shop there.
2. Posts that are put up on various social media sites.
3. Digital videos and pictures that are captured on our phones
4. Purchase transactions that are made through e-commerce.

These are just a few places where we are able to gather up some of the data that we need and put it to use with data science. And as the IoT grows and more data is created on a daily basis, it is likely that we are going to find even more sources that will help us to take on our biggest business problems. And this leads us to need data science more than ever.

All of this data that we are gathering from the sources above and more will be known as big data. Currently, most companies are going to be flooded and a bit overwhelmed by all of the data that is coming their way. This is why it is so important for these companies to have a good idea of what to do with the exploding amount of data and how they are able to utilize it to get ahead.

It is not enough to just gather up the data. This may seem like a great idea, but if you just gather up that data, and don't learn what is inside of it, then you are leading yourself to trouble. Once you can learn what information is inside of that data, and what it all means, you will find that it is much easier to use that information to give yourself the competitive advantage that you are looking for.

Data science is going to help us to get all of this done. It is designed to make it easier for us to really take in the big picture and use data for our needs. It will encompass all of the parts of the process of getting the data to work for us, from gathering the data to cleaning it up and organizing it, to analyzing it, to creating visuals to help us better understand the data, and even to the point of how we decide to use that data. All of this comes together and helps us to really see what is inside of the data, and it is all a part of the data science process.

Data science is going to work because it is able to bring together a ton of different skills, like statistics, mathematics, and business domain knowledge and can help out a company in many ways. Some of the things that data science is able to do when it is used in the proper manner, for a company will include some of the following:

1. Reduce costs
2. Get the company into a new market
3. Tap into a new demographic to increase their reach.

4. Gauge the effectiveness of a marketing campaign.
5. Launch a new service or a new product.

And this is just the start of the list. If you are willing to work with data science and learn the different steps that come with it, you will find that it is able to help your business out in many different manners, and it can be one of the best options for you to use in order to get ahead in your industry.

How Is Data Science Used?

One of the best ways to learn more about data science and how it works is to take a look at how some of the top players in the industry are already using data science. There are a ton of big-name companies who are already relying on data science to help them reach their customers better, keep waste and costs down, and so much more. For example, some of the names that we are going to take a look at here include Google, Amazon, and Visa.

As you will see with all of these, one of the biggest deciding factors for an organization is what value they think is the most important to extract from their data using analytics, and how they would like to present that information as well. Let's take a look at how each of these companies has been able to use data science for their needs to see some results.

First on the list is Google. This is one of the biggest companies right now that is on a hiring spree for trained data scientists. Google has been driven by data science in a lot of the work that they do, and they also rely on machine learning and artificial intelligence in order to reach their customers and to ensure that they are providing some of the best products possible to customers as well. Data science and some good analysis have been able to help them get all of this done effectively.

Next on the list is the company Amazon. This is a huge company known around the world, one that many of us use on a daily basis. It is a cloud computing and e-commerce site that relies heavily on data scientists to help them release new products, keep customer information safe, and even to do things like providing recommendations on what to purchase next on the site. They will use the data scientist to help them found out more about the mindset of the customer, and to enhance the geographical reach of their cloud domain and their e-commerce, just to name a few of their business goals right now.

And then we need to take a look at the Visa company and what they are doing with the help of data science. As an online financial gateway for countless other companies, Visa ends up completing transactions that are worth hundreds of millions in one day, much more than what other companies can even dream about. Due to a large number of transactions that are going on, Visa needs data scientists to help them increase their revenue, check if there are any fraudulent transactions, and even to customize some products and services based on the requirements of the customer.

The Lifecycle of Data Science

We are going to go into more detail about the lifecycle of data science as we progress through this guidebook, but first, we can take a moment to just look at some of the basics and see how we are able to use this for our own needs. Data science is going to follow our data from the gathering stage of the data, all the way through until we use that data to make our big business decisions. There are a number of steps that are going to show up in the process in the meantime, and being prepared to handle all of these, and all that they entail, is the challenge that comes when we want to rely on data science. Some of the basic steps that are found in the data science lifecycle are going to include:

1. Figuring out what business question we would like to answer with this process.
2. Gathering up the raw data to use.
3. Cleaning and organizing all of the unstructured data that we would like to use.
4. Preprocessing our data.

5. Creating a model with the help of machine learning and taking some time to train and test it to ensure accurate results along the way.
6. Running our data through the model to help us understand what insights and predictions are inside.
7. Use visuals to help us better understand the complex relationships that are found in any data that we are using for this analysis.

While the steps may sound easy enough to work with, there are going to be some complexities and a lot of back and forth that we have to work with here. The most important thing here is to go into it without any preconceived notions of what you would like to see happen and don't try to push your own agenda on the data. This is the best way to ensure that you will actually learn what is inside of that data and can make it easier to choose the right decisions for your needs as well.

The Components of Data Science

Now, we also need to take some time to look at the basics of data science. There are going to be a few key components that come into play when we are talking about data science, and having these in place is going to make a big difference in how well we are able to handle some of the different parts that come with data science, and how we can take on some of the different parts that we need with our own projects. Some of the key components that we need to take a look at when it comes to data science will include:

1. The various types of data: The foundation of any data science project is going to be the raw set of data. There are a lot of different types. We can work with the structured data that is mostly found in tabular form, and the unstructured data, which is going to include PDF files, emails, videos, and images.

2. Programming: You will need some kind of programing language to get the work done, with Python and R being the best option. Data management and data analysis are going to be

done with some computer programming. Python and R are the two most popular programming languages that we will focus on here.

3. Statistics and probability. Data is going to be manipulated in different ways in order to extract some good information out of it. The mathematical foundation of data science is going to be probability and statistics. Without having a good knowledge of the probability and statistics, there is going to be a higher possibility of misinterpreting the data and reaching conclusions that are not correct. This is a big reason why the probability and statistics that we are looking at here are going to be so important in data science.

4. Machine learning: As someone who is working with data science, each day you are going to spend at least a little time learning the algorithms of machine learning. This can include methods of classification and regression. It is important for a data scientist to know machine learning to complete their job since this is the tool that is needed to help predict valuable insights from the data that is available.

5. Big data: In our current world, raw data is going to be what we use to train and test our models, and then figure out the best insights and predictions out of that data. Working with big data is able to help us to figure out what important, although hidden, information is found in our raw data. There are a lot of different tools that we are able to use in order to help us not only find the big data but also to process some of these big data as well.

There are many companies that are learning the value of data science and all that is going to come with it. They like the idea that they can take all of the data they have been collecting for a long period of time and put it to use to increase their business and give them that competitive edge they have been looking for. In the rest of this guidebook, we are going to spend some time focusing on how to work with data science and all of the different parts that come with it as well.

Chapter 2: The Basics of the Python Language

One of the best coding languages that you are able to work with when you want to start handling your own data science project is the Python language. This is a fantastic language that is able to take on all of the work that you want to do with data science and has the power that is needed to help create some great machine learning algorithms. With that said, it is still a great option for beginners because it has been designed to work with those who have never done programming before. While you can choose to work with the R programming language as well, you will find that the Python language is one of the best options because of its ease of use and power that combines together.

Before we dive into how Python is able to work with some of the things that you would like to do with data science, we first need to take some time to look at the basics of the Python language first. Python is a great language to look through, and you will be able to learn how to do some of the codings that you need to in no time. Some of the different types of coding that you can do with the Python language will include:

The Statements

The first thing that we are going to take a moment to look through when it comes to our Python language is the keywords. This is going to focus on the lines or sentences that you would like to have the compiler show up on your screen. You will need to use some of the keywords that we will talk about soon, and then you can tell the compiler what statements to put up on the screen. If you would like to leave a message on the screen such as what we can do with the Hello, World! The program, you will need to use that as your statement, and the print keyword, so the complier knows how to behave.

The Python Operators

We can also take some time to look at what is known as the Python operators. These are often going to get ignored when it comes time to write out codes because they don't seem like they are that important. But if you skip out on writing them, they are going to really make it so that your code will not work the way that you would like. There are a number of different types of Python operators that we are able to focus on, so making sure that you know what each kind is all about, and when to add these into your code, will make a world of difference as well.

Operators are pretty simple parts of your code, but you should still know how they work. You will find that there are actually a few different types of them that work well. For example, the arithmetic functions are great for helping you to add, divide, subtract, and multiply different parts of the code together. There are assignment operators that will assign a specific value to your variable so that the compiler knows how to treat this. There are also comparison operators that will allow you to look at a few different pieces of code and then determine if they are similar or not and how the computer should react based on that information.

The Keywords

The keywords are another important part of our Python code that we need to take a look at. These are going to be the words that we need to reserve because they are responsible for giving the compiler the instructions or the commands that you would like for it to use. These key words ensure that the code is going to perform the way that you would like it to the whole time.

These keywords need to be reserved, so make sure that you are not using them in the wrong places. If you do not use these keywords in the right manner, or you don't put them in the right place, then the compiler is going to end up with some issues understanding what you would like it to do, and you will not be able to get the results that you want. Make sure to learn the important keywords that come with the Python language and learn how to put them in the right spot of your code to get the best results with it.

Working with Comments

As we work with the Python coding, there are going to be times when we need to spend our time working with something that is known as a comment. This is going to be one of the best things that we are able to do in order to make sure that we can name a part of the code, or when we want to leave a little note for yourself or for another programmer, then you are going to need to work with some of the comments as well.

These comments are going to be a great option to work with. They are going to allow you to really leave a nice message in the code, and the compiler will know that it should just skip over that part of the code, and not read through it at all. It is as simple as that and can save you a lot of hassle and work inside of any code you are doing.

So, any time that you would like to write out a comment inside of your Python code, you just need to use the # symbol, and then the compiler will know that it is supposed to skip over that part of the code and not read it. We are able to add in as many of these comments as we would like into the code. Just remember to keep these to the number that is necessary, rather than going overboard with this, because it ensures that we are going to keep the code looking as nice and clean as possible.

The Python Class

One thing that is extremely important when it comes to working with Python, and other similar languages, is the idea that the language is separated out into classes and objects. The objects are meant to fit into the classes that you create, giving them more organization and ensuring that the different parts are going to fit together the way that you would like without a trouble. In some of the older types of programming languages, the organization was not there, and this caused a lot of confusion and frustration for those who were just starting out.

These classes are simply going to be a type of container that can hold onto your objects, the ones that you write out and are based on actual items in the real world and other parts of the code. You will need to make sure that you name these classes in the right manner, and then have them listed out in the code in the right spot to make sure they actually work and call up the objects that you need. And placing the right kinds of objects into the right class is going to be important as well.

You can store anything that you want inside a class that you design, but you must ensure that things that are similar end up in the same class. The items don't have to be identical to each other, but when someone takes a look at the class that you worked on, they need to be able to see that those objects belong together and make sense to be together.

For example, you don't have to just put cars into the same class, but you could have different vehicles in the same class. You could have items that are considered food. You can even have items that are all the same color. You get some freedom when creating the classes and storing objects in those classes, but when another programmer looks at the code, they should be able to figure out what the objects inside that class are about and those objects should share something in common.

Classes are very important when it comes to writing out your code. These are going to hold onto the various objects that you write in the code and can ensure that everything is stored properly. They will also make it easier for you to call out the different parts of your code when you need them for execution.

How to Name Your Identifiers

Inside the Python language, there are going to be a number of identifiers that we need to spend some time on. Each of these identifiers is going to be important, and they are going to make a big difference in some of the different parts of the code that you are able to work with. They are going to come to us under a lot of different names, but you will find that they are going to follow the same kinds of rules when it comes to naming them, and that can make it a lot easier for a beginner to work with as well.

To start with, you can use a lot of different types of characters in order to handle the naming of the identifiers that you would like to work with. You are able to use any letter of the alphabet that you would like, including uppercase and lowercase, and any combination of the two that you would like. Using numbers and the underscore symbol is just fine in this process as well.

With this in mind, there are going to be a few rules that you have to remember when it comes to naming your identifiers. For example, you are not able to start out a name with the underscore symbol or with a number. So, writing something like 3puppies or _threepuppies would not work. But you can do it with something like threepuppies for the name. A programmer also won't be able to add in spaces between the names either. You can write out threepuppies or three_puppies if you would like, but do not add the space between the two of them.

In addition to some of these rules, we need to spend some time looking at one other rule that is important to remember. Pick out a name for your identifier that is easy to remember and makes sense for that part of the code. This is going to ensure that you are able to understand the name and that you will be able to remember it later on when you need to call it up again.

Python Functions

Another topic that we are going to take a quick look at here as we work with the Python language is the idea of the Python functions. These are going to be a set of expressions that can also be statements inside of your code as well. You can have the choice to give them a name or let them remain anonymous. They are often the first-class objects that we are able to explore as well, meaning that your restrictions on how to work with them will be lower than we will find with other class objects.

Now, these functions are very diversified and there are many attributes that you can use when you try to create and bring up those functions. Some of the choices that you have with these functions include:

- ___doc___: This is going to return the docstring of the function that you are requesting.
- Func_default: This one is going to return a tuple of the values of your default argument.
- Func_globals: This one will return a reference that points to the dictionary holding the global variables for that function.

- Func_dict: This one is responsible for returning the namespace that will support the attributes for all your arbitrary functions.
- Func_closure: This will return to you a tuple of all the cells that hold the bindings for the free variables inside of the function.

There are different things that you can do with your functions, such as passing it as an argument over to one of your other functions if you need it. Any function that is able to take on a new one as the argument will be considered the higher-order function in the code. These are good to learn because they are important to your code as you move.

The Importance of Variables

While we are working with the Python programming language, we are going to run across sometimes when we need to work with the Python variables. These are going to be spaces in the memory of our computer that are able to hold spaces for the different values that are in any code that we are writing. This makes it easier for the code to pull up what is needed at the right times, simply by calling up the variable that we ask for as well.

Assigning a value to a variable is a pretty easy process. We just need to name the variable and then use the equal sign in order to get it all done. As long as the equal sign is in between the two, your compiler is going to know which value is going to be assigned back to which variable that is in the system. And if you would like to assign more than one value to a single variable, you would just need to make sure that there is an equal sign that falls in between all of that as well.

As we can see with some of the different parts that we have just looked through in this guidebook, learning how to work with the Python coding language is a great option to work with as well. Even if you have never spent any time working with coding in the past, and you are looking to just get into it in order to learn how to work with data science and one of these projects for your company, make sure to check out this chapter to get started.

Chapter 3: Why Use Python for Data Science?

Now that we know a bit about some of the basics of the Python language, it is time to take a look at how Python is going to be important and helpful when it comes to working with data science. We already know a lot about data science and why it is important for the company and helping you to open up a lot of opportunities to beat out the competition and meet your customer needs better than ever before. Now it is time to take a look at why the Python coding language is going to be one of the best options to use to help you get work done with data science.

The Python language is one of the best options to work with when it is time to handle the data science project that you would like to do. There are a ton of projects that you are able to handle with data science, and Python is able to take on even the more complex problems that you are trying to handle. There are many reasons why Python is going to be the best option to help you get all of this done, including:

This language, even though there are a lot of complexities that come with it, is easy for a lot of beginners to learn. If you are just beginning with coding to help out with data science and you are worried about getting started, you will find that Python is the perfect one to choose from. It is designed to be as easy to work with as possible, and even those who have never done anything with coding ever will find that working with Python is not as bad as it may seem in the beginning.

The whole point of working with Python is to make coding as simple as possible, even for those who have never done coding in the past. You will find that the syntax, the English words that are used, and the fact that it is an object oriented coding language means that this kind of language is going to be as easy to do as possible.

There is still a lot of power that comes with the Python language, even though it is designed for a beginner to learn to code for the first time. Many people worry that when they get started with the Python language that it is going to be too simplistic. They may reason that because this kind of language is designed to help beginners get started with their work, it is going to be too simple in order to get any of the more complex codes done and ready to go.

This can't be further from the truth. You will find that working with Python is a great option, even with the ease of use, that is strong enough to handle some of the more complex codes and projects that you would like to get done. For example, Python is able to help out, with the right libraries and extensions, things like machine learning, deep learning, science, mathematics, and other complicated processes, whether they are needed for data science or not.

More productivity for the programmer: The Python language has a lot of designs that are object-oriented and a lot of support libraries. Because of all these resources and how easy it is to use the program; the programmer is going to increase their productivity. This can even be used to help improve the productivity of the programmer while using languages like C#, C++, C, Perl, VB, and even Java.

When it is time for you to work on some of the different parts of your data science project, having more of that productivity is going to be so important overall. You will find that when the programmer is able to get more things done in a shorter amount of time, it ensures that they are going to see a big difference in the project they are working with.

Integration features: Python can be great because it integrates what is known as the Enterprise Application Integration. This really helps with a lot of the different things you want to work on in Python including COBRA, COM, and more. It also has some powerful control capabilities as it calls directly through Java, C++, and C. Python also has the ability to process XML and other markup languages because it can run all of the modern operating systems, including Windows, Mac OS X, and Linux through the same kind of byte code.

While we are focusing mainly on how you can use the Python language to help you with your data science project, there are some data science libraries that are going to need some compatibility with other programming languages to get the work done and to handle your algorithm. This is why Python is such an amazing language to work with. It is compatible with a lot of different languages, which means that you will be able to use all of the libraries and extensions that you would like to focus on and still have it work with the other languages that are required.

The large community that comes with Python is going to make it a lot easier for you to get the help that is needed as you work through the codes, or if you get stuck on anything you are doing. There are a lot of complex codes that we need to focus on when we work with data science, even with the help of the Python coding language. If we get stuck, it can sometimes be hard to go through and actually figure out what is going wrong and how to make it better.

The community that comes with Python is going to help to make this a lot easier to work with. You will be able to find a bunch of other programmers, some of whom have been using Python for a long time, who will be able to offer you advice, provide you with some helpful codes, and can get you out of the issues that you are dealing with when it comes to a data science project.

The standard library that comes with Python has a lot of power that you need in order to get many of your coding tasks down. Just by downloading the Python language, you are going to get a fantastic library that is able to handle a lot of the work that you want to do with Python overall, and a lot of the topics that you would like to handle as well. While you will need to add in a few extensions to help you attempt machine learning and some of the models that you need with data science, you will find that the standard library of Python is able to handle a lot of the work that you want.

For example, when you are working with the Python language and the standard library that comes with it, you will be able to write loops, inheritances, conditional statements, and so much more. All of these can come into play, even when you work with some of the more complex parts that happen with machine learning and data science.

There are a lot of special extensions and libraries that we are able to do with Python that is perfect for data science and machine learning. Even though there is a lot that we are able to do when it comes to using the Python language to help out just with the standard library, there are also a number of libraries that work not only with Python, but also help us to get more done with data science at the same time.

We are going to take some time to look at a lot of the different libraries for data science and Python, and you will get a chance to see how well these can help out with some of your data science projects. Some of the best options though, based on which machine learning algorithms you want to work with, include TensorFlow, Scikit-Learn, NumPy, SciPy, and Pandas.

Python is one of the options that is used to help out with creating the machine learning algorithms that you need to create your own models with data science. Without these models, you are going to end up having trouble going through all of that data you have been able to collect and actually find the insights and predictions that you want from that data. There are other languages you can use, most notably the R programming language, but Python is one of the best to help get all of this done.

There are a number of steps that come with working on your own data science projects, but in one part, the analysis part, we need to be able to use machine learning, deep learning, and some other techniques to help us to create a model that can handle the data that we are working with. Going through that data is going to take a long time if you try to do it manually. But with the right model with the Python language, we are going to be able to sort through that information and get those insights and predictions out of this data faster than ever before.

And this is one of the main points of working with data science on the first point. We want to be able to take all of that raw data that we have collected over time, and then figure out what hidden insights are found inside of there. The models that we are able to create with the help of machine learning and Python can really help us to meet these goals and will ensure that we are able to get ahead of the competition, meet the needs of our customers, and more.

There are a lot of reasons why a data scientist will want to work with the Python language. There may be a few other coding languages that are out there that you are able to use, but thanks to all of the reasons that we have discussed above, and more, we are able to see that working with the Python language is one of the best options to work with that can help you create the models that you need, work with a variety of libraries that help with machine learning, and so much more.

Chapter 4: The Best Python Libraries for Data Science, and How They Can Help Get the Job Done

The next thing that we need to take some time to look through is some of the best libraries that we are able to use when it comes to working with the Python language and data science. The standard Python library is able to do a lot of amazing things. But when it is time to make some of the models that you would like with machine learning and more, the standard library is going to lack a few of the capabilities that you would like to work with.

This is why we would need to bring in some additional extensions and libraries to the mix. You will find that Python is going to have a lot of different libraries that will be able to handle some of the data science and the different models that you want to handle overall. You just need to pick out which one is going to work for the projects you have in mind. Some are able to help out with all of the different types of tasks that you want to handle, and some are going to do better with certain algorithms or models that we want to work with.

These libraries are going to be critical when it is time to handle the algorithms and the models that are needed. Without them, you are going to miss out on some of the tasks that are needed to help with data science, and it will make it more difficult to create models that help you with predictions and more. There are a lot of different libraries that you are able to work with when it is time to handle machine learning, deep learning, and data science. Some of the best libraries to help you get all of the tasks with these models done as efficiently as possible will include:

NumPy

When we first get started with doing some data science on Python, one of the best libraries to download is going to be NumPy. Many of the other data science libraries are going to rely on some of the capabilities that come with this kind of library, so having it set up and ready to go on your computer is going to make a big difference.

When you are ready to start working with some of the scientific tasks with Python, you are going to need to work with the Python SciPy Stack. This is going to be a collection of software that is specifically designed to help us complete some of the scientific computing that we need to do with Python. Keep in mind that this SciPy stack is not going to be the same thing as the SciPy library though so keep the two of these apart. The stack is going to be pretty big because there are more than 12 libraries that are found inside of it, and we want to put a focal point on the core package, particularly the most essential ones that help with data science.

The most fundamental package around which this computation stack is going to be built around is NumPy, which is going to stand for Numerical Python. It is going to provide us with an abundance of useful features for operations that you want to handle with matrices and n-arrays. This library is going to help us with a lot of different tasks that we want to do, including the vectorization of mathematical operations on the NumPy array type, which is going to ameliorate the performance and will speed up the execution that we see at the same time.

SciPy

Another library that we need to spend some time working with is known as SciPy. This is going to be a library of software that can help us to handle some of the different tasks that we have for science and engineering. SciPy is going to contain some of the modules that we need to help with statistics, optimization integration, and even linear algebra to name a few of the tasks that we are able to do with it.

The main functionality that we are able to get when we use the SciPy library is going to be built upon the NumPy library that we talked about before. This means that the arrays that are found in SciPy are going to make quite a bit of use of the NumPy library. It is going to provide some efficient numerical routines as numerical integrations, optimization, and a lot of other options through the specific submodules. The functions of all of this inside of this library are going to be well documented also.

Pandas

The third library that we are going to look at is one of the best options that we are able to use with data science. It is designed in order to help with all the different steps that you need to do with data science, such as collecting the data, sorting through and processing all of that data that we have, analyzing it, and even making some of the visualizations that we need along with this kind of language.

This library is going to be a package that comes with Python that has been specifically designed in order to make some work with the relational and the labeled data both the kind that is simple and intuitive. Pandas are going to be the perfect tool to help out with a lot of different processes that we would like to handle, including data wrangling. In addition, it is going to work well for quick and easy data visualization, aggregation, and manipulation, along with any of the other tasks that we want to get done with data science.

Matplotlib

As you are working through some of the projects that you would like to do with data science, there is going to come a time when you need to handle data visualization. This is going to ensure that we are able to handle all of the information and the complex relationships that show up in any data that we are working with. Often our minds are going to be able to understand the data that is in front of us a lot better when it is in a visual, rather than trying to read through all of the information. This is why the visualization process of data is so important when it comes to working with data science. And that is why we are going to take a bit of time to look at some of the different Python extensions and libraries that we are able to use that help us take all of our data and create the visuals that we need.

The first option for this is Matplotlib. This is a library that has been created in order to help us make some simple and powerful visualizations in no time. it is actually a top-notch piece of software that is making Python, with some help from the other three libraries that we have been talking about so far in this guidebook. It is also a very good competitor to some of the other big names in graphing and visualization libraries out there, including Mathematica and MATLAB.

However, we have to remember that with this library, it is considered pretty low-level. This means that you are going to need to write out more code to help us reach more advanced levels of visualization and get the results that we would like. This means that with this library, we are going to need to put in some more effort to complete some of the tasks that we want to be compared to the higher-level tools, but for many programmers, it is worth it.

With this library, we are able to handle pretty much any kind of visualization that we would like to do with the data we have been able to collect. Some of the visualizations that are available with this kind of library, with the help of the Python language, will include:

1. Line plots
2. Scatter plots
3. Bar charts and histograms
4. Pie charts
5. Spectrograms
6. Quiver plots
7. Contour plots
8. Stem plots

There are also a few capabilities that happen with this kind of language that is going to help us to create labels, legends, and grids, along with a few other formatting entities that can help us get the visuals that we want. That is what is so neat about this library, we are able to customize everything that we want inside of it to get the visuals that we need.

Scikit-Learn

This is going to be an additional package that you are able to get along with the SciPy Stack that we talked about earlier on. This one was designed to help us out with a few specific functions, like image processing and facilitation of machine learning. When it comes to the latter of the two, one of the most prominent is going to be this library compared to all of the others. It is also one that is built on SciPy and will make a lot of use on a regular basis of the math operations that come with SciPy as well.

This package is a good one to work with because it can expose a concise and consistent interface that programmers are able to use when it is time to work with the ones that go with the most common algorithms of machine learning. This is going to make it simple to bring machine learning into the production system. The library is able to combine together quality code and good documentation, which can bring together high performance and ease of use, and it is one of the industry standards when it comes to doing anything that you need with machine learning in Python.

Theano

Theano is the next library that we can take a look at, and it is going to spend some more time working with a process known as deep learning, rather than all about machine learning. Theano is going to be a package from Python that will define some of the multi-dimensional arrays, similar to what we see with the NumPy library above, along with some of the math operations and expressions.

This particular library is compiled, which makes sure that it is going to run as efficiently as possible on all architectures that you choose along the way. it was originally developed by the Machine Learning group of University de Montreal, and it is going to be used to help us handle a lot of the applications that we want to complete in machine learning.

The most important thing that we need to look at when it comes to working on this library is that Theano is able to tightly integrate together with the NumPy library on some of the operations that are lower level. The library is also going to optimize the use of CPU and GPU when you are working, which ensures that the performance that we will see with data-intensive computation is even faster than before. The stability and the efficiency that come with this library are going to allow us to receive more precise results, even when we are talking about values that are smaller.

TensorFlow

We can't finish off a discussion about the different libraries that are offered with the Python language without also taking a look at the TensorFlow library. This is a special library because it is one that was developed by Google and it is an open-sourced library of data flow graph computations, and more that are sharpened to make sure that they do some of the work that we want with machine learning. Originally, this was a library that was designed in order to meet some of the requirements of high demand that the Google environment has to work with on a regular basis.

In addition, we will find that this library is a great one to help us work with the training of neural networks, which is one of the best types of machine learning algorithms that we are able to work with when it comes to handling our data and making decisions through a system. However, we have to remember that TensorFlow is not strictly for scientific use in the borders of Google. It has enough power, and it is considered a more general-purpose enough to help us with a lot of real-world applications.

One of the key features that we are able to focus on when we work with this library is that it comes with a multi-layered nodes system. This is a good thing to work with because it is going to enable us to quickly train our artificial neural networks, even when we are working with a very large set of data. This is going to help us with a lot of great algorithms and models that we want to create. For example, this kind of library has been able to help us power the voice recognition of Google and object identification from pictures to name a few uses.

Keras

And the final library that we are going to take a look at in this guidebook is the Keras library. This is going to be a great open-sourced library that is going to help again with some of the neural networks that we want to handle in this language, especially the ones that happen at a higher level, and it is also written in Python to make things easier. We will find that when it comes to the Keras library, the whole thing is pretty easy to work with and minimalistic, with some high-level extensibility to help us out. it is going to use the TensorFlow or Theano libraries as the back end, but right now Microsoft is working to integrate it with CNTK as a new back end to give us some more options.

Many users are going to enjoy some of the minimalistic design that comes with Keras. In fact, this kind of design is aimed at making our experimentation as easy and fast as well, because the systems that you will use will still stay compact. In addition, we will find that Keras is going to be an easy language to get started with, and it can make some of the prototyping that we want to handle easier.

We will also find that the Keras library is going to be written out in pure Python, and it is going to be a higher level just by nature, helping us to get more programming and machine learning done on our own. It is also highly extendable and modular. Despite the ease of using this library, the simplicity that comes with it, and the high-level orientation, Keras is still going to have enough power to help us get a lot of serious modeling.

The general idea that is going to come with Keras is based on lots of layers, and then everything else that you need for that model is going to be built around all of the layers. The data is going to be prepared in tensors. The first layer that comes with this is then responsible for the input of those tensors. Then the last layer however many layers this may be down the road, is going to be responsible for the output. We will find that all of the other parts of the model are going to be built in between on this to help us get the results that we would like.

As we can see, there are a lot of different libraries that we are able to handle with the help of Python that can also help us get some work done with data science and machine learning. Creating some of the models that we need in order to see success with machine learning, and to ensure that we can take all of the raw data that we have gathered over time and actually use it and make good business decisions, is impossible without some of these Python libraries around to help us get it done.

All of the libraries that we have talked about in this guidebook are going to handle different parts of the process and can help us out in a variety of manners as well along the way. we need to be able to pick out which library is the best one for us, and then move on from there when it is time to use the Python language to create the models that are the most important for our needs. And the different libraries that we have discussed in this guidebook are going to be just the tools that we need to get the work done.

Chapter 5: The Basics for the Data Life Cycle

One of the most important things that we are able to do when it is time to combine data science and Python together into one is learning a bit more about the data life cycle. There are a lot of steps that we need to take before we are able to take our data and actually learn something from it. Many people and companies who want to get into the process of using their data to make decisions assume that they can just look around for a bit of data, and then find the insights all at once.

As we are going to explore in this chapter, there are actually a number of steps that need to be taken in order to actually gain the insights that you would like from all of that data you were able to collect. This is a process that takes some time, and sometimes it is not as simple or as quick as we would like. However, taking your time and going through all of the steps that we are going to talk about in this chapter will make a world of difference when it comes to the results that you are able to get. Let's take a look at some of the main steps that companies need to follow in the life cycle of their data to ensure they get the best results possible:

Gathering our Data

The first thing that we need to do is go and find all of that data that we would like to use in the first place. This is going to be a critical step because we are not going to be able to create a model and learn a lot of the predictions and the insights that we would like if there isn't any data for us to sort through in the first place. This is a very important step to take because it ensures that we not only have a lot of data, but we also have the data that we would like to use to really find the answers to our biggest questions.

To start with, we need to be able to go through and figure out what business question we would like to have answered. We are not just randomly looking through some of the data that is there and hoping that we can figure out something. We have way too much data to sort through when it comes to this, and it is not going to end well for us if we are doing this. Instead, we need to spend some time thinking about what our biggest business problems are, and what we would like to gain when we go through this data.

Each company is going to have their own ideas when it comes to gathering the data and getting things set up here. The biggest business problem for you may not be the same challenge that another company is going through. So, make sure that you take a look at your own business and figure out what you would like to improve. Do you want to reach your customers better or give them a better experience? Do you want to reduce waste and increase your profits? Do you want to find a new demographic or niche that you would like to enter? These are all things that you are able to consider when it is time to start looking at the business problem you would like to fix, and when it is time to look through your data for answers.

In this step, we are going to get busy doing some research. We need to spend some time looking for some of the information that you would like to do. There are a lot of different places where you are able to look for the data, but it is going to depend on what business problem you would like to be able to solve. You may find that looking on social media, checking out the responses that you have gotten from customers in the past, looking at surveys, and more can be a great way to help you to see the results that you would like.

During this time, we also need to do some assessing as well. It is important to know whether you already have the right kinds of resources to take on this project, or if there is something that you are missing and need to fill in ahead of time. you will need to assess whether you have the right resources in terms of people, time, data, and technology to help support that new project that you want to work with. in this phase, you may find that it is time to frame the business problem that you have, and then formulate the IH or initial hypotheses that you would like to work with.

Preparing the Data

The next thing that we need to spend some time on is preparing the data that we want to use. It is likely that you went through and collected the data that is going to be used in your model and some of your decisions, later on, are going to come from a variety of sources. And this is going to make things messy. The results that you get from a survey that you sent out are going to be different compared to the results that you get from your social media account.

Both of these can be really useful when it is time to work with data science, but they are going to present a few challenges to you, and this does mean that we need to be able to prepare the data and get it all cleaned and organized ahead of time to avoid confusion and to ensure that our model is able to handle it.

During this particular phase, we are going to need to work with something that is known as an analytical sandbox. This is a place where you are able to perform some of the different analytics that you want to use for the whole time that you handle your project. There is going to be a lot of steps that you need to handle while working on your data before you are ever able to do the modeling that we are going to focus on later on.

For example, during this stage, we are going to need to explore, preprocess, and then condition the data before we work with any of the modelings that happens. Further, we are going to need to work with what is known as the ETLT process to make sure that the raw data we were able to collect along the way is able to get into that sandbox so we are able to do the work that we would like with it.

Preparing the data is going to take some time. We need to be able to take it and make sure that all of the data is in the same format so that the model is better able to understand what we want to see happening. We also need to take care of any missing data or duplicate data, because this is likely to cause some issues with the work that we are doing in this process. Taking the time to prepare the data and get it as organized as possible during this step is going to be the key that we need to ensuring our model will work properly later on and give us the insights that we need.

Now, there are a few options that you can work with when it is time to prepare our data. The R and the Python programming languages are going to be great when it is time to work with cleaning, transformation, and visualization of our data, all of which are important aspects of our data science project. Using these tools is going to make it easier for us to manage our data and spot some of the outliers ahead of time while establishing a relationship between the variables as you go.

During this time, we are going to make sure that the data is as organized and as perfect as possible, ensuring that we get as much efficiency and accuracy out of our data as possible. Once we have been able to go through and clean and prepare the data that we are working with, it will then be time for us to move on to complete a bit of exploratory analytics on that data, and that is when we move on to the next step.

Model Planning

Once we have had some time to go through and collect our raw data and gather it up from all of the different sources that we want to use, and we have prepared and cleaned off the data so that it is ready to use, it is time for us to move on to the third phase of this process, that of model planning. In this phase, we are going to spend some time figuring out which techniques and methods are the best in order to draw the relationships between the variables.

These relationships are going to be important and we need to spend some time looking into them and understanding how they work a bit better. In fact, these relationships are going to be able to set up some of the bases that we need for our algorithms to work, and that is definitely going to affect the next phase as it is implemented. It is during this phase that we are able to apply the EDA or the Exploratory Data Analysis with the help of a lot of different visualization tools and the statistical formulas that we want to use in this process.

Now, the project that you want to complete is only going to be as good as the tools that you have to help you get all of this done. The three tools that are going to be imperative to helping you to plan out the code that you want to work with to help with your model include:

1. Python: As we have discussed throughout this guidebook already, Python is going to come with a lot of modeling capabilities and it is going to ensure that you have the kind of environment that you would like to help with some of the interpretive models and other things that you

want to work with. The R programming language is going to help out with this as well, you just need to get it set up and make sure that it is able to handle everything with the right libraries as well.

2. SQL Analysis services: This is the one that is able to perform some of the in-database analytics that you would like to use, ones that are going to be the most common when you are doing a variety of data mining functions and some predictive models that are basic in the beginning.

3. SAS/ACCESS: This is a tool that we are able to use when it is time to access the data that we want from Hadoop and it is used for helping us to create a model flow diagram that we are able to repeat the results with and that we are able to reuse any time that we will like.

These are just a few of the different tools that we are able to find when it is time to work with our own model planning process. The three above are some of the most common and are definitely options that we want to focus on because of the benefits that they can provide. But looking around and doing some of your own research is going to ensure that you are able to find the results that you want, and the right tools, in order to plan out that model and get it ready to handle some of the work that you want to do with that raw data.

Build the Model

Now that we have had a chance to talk about planning out the model, and some of the different tools and techniques that we are able to use in order to make this happen, it is time for us to go through and actually build up this model. This is a process that is going to take some time, and we need to make sure that we can spend our time training and testing the model as well, to ensure that it will provide us with some of the accurate results that we are looking for.

When we are working on this phase, we are going to work with two distinct data sets, one for training and one for testing. You will also need to take some time to do a bit of exploration to figure out whether or not the existing tools that we are using will be enough to help us run our models on it, or if we would like to work with a more robust environment in the process. You will need to take some time here to analyze the various learning techniques, including clustering, classification, and association to help us build up a model.

So, what we want to do here is take some of the data that we have and split it up into a training group and the testing group. The training group should be quite a bit larger than what we are going to see with the testing model because we want to feed the algorithm with a lot of different parts to ensure that it will work the way that we want.

With these two groups of our data set up and ready to go, we are going to feed through the training set to the model. This helps the model to learn what the input and the output should be so that it can make some accurate predictions and learn in the future. This is much like what we see in our classes with students receiving a lot of information from teaching to help them learn a specific topic.

After all of the training, data has gone through the model, it is time to test it. We are going to send through some more data, the data that we put aside into our testing data set, and then send this through, but without the correct answers or outputs going along with them. This is going to see how well the algorithm, or the model was able to learn in the first place. The goal is to get it as high as about 50 percent as possible.

Anything about 50 percent is going to show that the model is accurate, especially in the first run. It is assumed that is the model just took a look at the information and made a guess on the data, then it would likely be able to get the answers right half of the time. So, when the model is able to get higher than that 50 percent, it shows us that the model was actually able to learn from the training set that we used and that it is going to provide us with some more accurate results over time.

Of course, for the first round of this, the accuracy may not be that high, maybe in the 60 percent range. This is not a bad thing, but of course, we want to make sure that the accuracy is a bit higher before we start to rely on this to help us make important decisions for the business. The goal here is to then go through and do another set of training, and another testing, doing this a few times in order to increase that accuracy and help us get better results.

The more times that we are able to go through this process of training and testing, and the more that the model is able to learn along the way, the better the accuracy will become. You do not need to do the training and the testing until this model gets to 100 percent because that would take forever, and there is always a possibility of error so reaching that is impossible. But getting a bit higher with the predictions can be the key that you need to really help you to get this model ready to use on some of your own data as well.

Operationalize

Now that the model has had some time to be built up and we are sure that the information that it provides us, such as the predictions and the insights that we are hoping to use, are as accurate as possible, it is time for us to use the model to help us out. Here we can take some time to put in our data and let the model do its work helping us to see the predictions and insights that are going to come out of that data as well.

In this phase, we are going to gather up the insights and the predictions that we need, and then use them as a way to make some important decisions for the business. It is important here to work with the technical documents, code, briefings and final reports on the findings that you were able to get out of the process.

In some cases, this is going to be taken a bit further. Depending on the business process that you would like to work with, it may help to do a pilot project, one that we are able to implement in real-time, to help us learn whether the insights and the predictions that we get out of this model are good for us, or if they need some adjustments before we implement them throughout the whole company. This is going to still be a part of the process because we can use these findings to help bolster up some of the other parts that we want to work with.

When we work with one of these pilot projects, it helps us to see the work of the model in a clear picture and to see some of the performance, as well as real-life constraints on a smaller scale, before we try to deploy it throughout the whole business. For example, sometimes a project or an idea may sound like a great thing to work with, but once you start to implement it, even on a smaller scale, things are going to start falling apart, and you can quickly see that the project or the idea that was there, is really bad and will cost too much money, or just won't work.

This isn't to say that the information and the predictions that you get form your model is going to be bad ones and that you shouldn't try them. Often the predictions and insights, as long as you did them in the proper manner with the model, are going to be really good for your business. They may have a few minor issues that can be ironed out, but these are not going to prevent you from taking those ideas and using them on a bigger scale over time. They are simply going to be a way to help you try something out, iron the wrinkles ahead of time, and then implement it on a larger scale when you are ready to proceed.

For example, let's say that you are working on a way to reduce waste in your company. You see that there is a new process that you can try, but you want to see how it is going to work before it becomes something big that you try to use. You work it out in one department, having the employees in that area try out the new rule and report back on how it works. You can quickly see whether there are any problems that are going to show up with this, and can then make the changes, or make the decision on whether or not to keep it, before putting in a lot of time and money to add this to the whole business at the same time.

Communicate the Results

The final step that we need to take a look at here is to communicate the results that we are seeing. We have gone through a lot of steps already with our data and with some of the machine learning algorithms that we want to focus on. And we have made some good headway in the process as well. Now that we know some of these insights, and perhaps even have a good idea of whether some of them are going to work in real life or not, it is time to actually communicate the results.

It is unlikely that the data scientist or the one who is actually going through all of this process and creating and working with the algorithms will be the one who uses that information. Instead, they are supposed to find that information and then present it to some of the key decision-makers in the company in order to help those top people figure things out. And that is exactly where this step of the process is going to come into play.

Now it is important to take some time in this part of the process to evaluate what information we were able to find inside of the data, and then evaluate if we have been able to achieve the goals that we would have liked to meet in the first stage of this process.

So, for this last phase that we are on right now, it is our goal to go through and identify all of the various key findings that showed up in the data that we have, and in all of the information that we are working with, and figure out how to communicate all of this information to the key stakeholders. Then together, or with just the key people who make decisions for that business, you will be able to determine whether or not the results that were found in the project were actually a success or failure.

Do not just focus on the information and the insights that were found int his process. Sure, those were important, but we need to determine whether this was a success or a failure in the process, and the decision here is going to be based completely on the criteria that we were able to develop in the first step. Writing that down in the very beginning can make it a lot easier to figure out what is going on here and whether your process was as successful as you thought.

As you are going through this, it is important to layout your findings in a clear and concise manner that is easy for others to understand. For example, you do not want to just push the data at them and say "good luck". This is not going to help anyone and could end up making it take way too long to find those insights. There are a number of methods that you are able to use in order to present the data that you want to work with, and taking the time to figure out which one is the best for you is going to be important to this process.

Writing out spreadsheets and reports on the data is very important and a good place to start, but we are able to take this a bit further. For most data scientists, when they get to this part of the process, it is a good idea to add in some visuals and more to help explain what the findings were for them. We already talked about one or two libraries that work with Python and data science that are able to help you create some of these important visuals, so you should have a lot of the tools that are needed to get started with that.

These visuals are going to make it a lot easier for those making decisions based on this data to really see some of the more complex relationships that are found in the data. It is much easier to take a look at a chart or a graph and see what is going on in the data than to spend a lot of time reading through spreadsheets and reports on the data. The latter should definitely spend some time in your thoughts and should come with the visuals so that others can double check your findings and to make you more reputable. But it is also best if we are able to focus on the visuals because these are much easier for most people to read through and understand overall.

As we can see, the process and all of the steps that come with a data science project are going to be complex and include a lot of work. And that is why the data scientist is in such high demand for many companies across a wide variety of industries right now. Those who are able to go through these steps, rather quickly and efficiently, will be valuable to the companies who are ready to start adding in some data science to their business.

The overall goal though of this is to make sure that we are able to focus on finding the best insights and predictions that will put our company ahead of the rest. There is a lot of competition, and the steps above are going to help us to find the information that backs our best decisions, and help us to beat out others in the industry. It may seem like a lot of steps, but it is definitely necessary to take all of that raw data that we have gathered and turn it into something that we are able to utilize and gain some benefit from in the long run.

Chapter 6: What is Data Mining?

While we are on the topic of the different steps that need to be taken along with data science, it is important to take a closer look at data mining and what it is all about. This is a specific part of the data science process that we need to focus on, and we are going to spend some time in this chapter looking into data mining, and all of the different parts that come with it. So, with that in mind, let's take a look at what data mining is all about, why it is so important to the process of data science overall, and why we would want to use it in the first place.

Our first goal is to learn a bit more about data mining and what this process is all about. Data mining is basically the steps that a company is able to use in order to take their raw data and then turn it into useful information. It is going to be more of a specialized form of the steps that we talked about in the previous chapter. With the help of machine learning, Python, and some specialized software, the company is able to use data mining in order to look for patterns that may show up n large batches of data.

The goal of looking through all of this data, and there is often quite a bit of that data that we need to go through in the first place, is to help a business learn more about their customers, beat out the competition, and even develop some better marketing strategies that will get them ahead in the industry. Some companies are also going to work with the steps of data mining in order to increase their sales, decrease costs, figure out which products to sell, and more.

There are a lot of things that need to come together if we would like to make sure our data mining process is going to work the way that we would like. Some of the steps that we need to look for when working on the data mining process includes an effective amount of data collection, warehousing, and processing power on our computer or system.

How Does Data Mining Work?

With some of the information above in mind, we now need to move on to some of the basics of how data mining is going to work. Data mining is going to involve a company exploring and then analyzing a large amount of information, in the hopes of gleaning some important and meaningful patterns and trends out of the whole thing. As we can imagine, when a company spends their time collecting a large amount of information, it is likely that they are going to be able to find a ton of insights and other valuable information inside.

There are a lot of ways that these companies are going to be able to use this information, including managing the credit risk of someone who wants to borrow money, database marketing, detecting fraud, filtering out spam emails, and even to figure out some of the opinions and sentiment of users on that system. All of these can be used in order to benefit your company and help you to get the advantage that you are looking for.

Of course, we need to take the enormous process of data mining and figure out how to break it down into easy steps that we are able to follow. For this to work, we are going to break it down into five steps that are easy to work with and can help us to get the best results.

The first step of this process is that the company is going to go through and collect the data that they need, and then load it up into the warehouse, or another storage area, that they want to use to keep ahold of that information. The type of data that you want to collect is going to be based on what information you would like, and what your overall goal is when you get started with this process as well.

The second step is that we would like to make sure that we are storing and managing the data in the right manner. This is usually going to be done either through the cloud or with some servers that the company is using on their own. Management teams, business analysts, and information technology professionals are then able to access the data and determine the best method that they can use in order to organize all of that data and learn more information from it.

Then, the company needs to go through and figure out what kind of application software they want to use. There are a number of these that are available for the programmer to choose from, and they can often work with machine learning and the Python coding language to help get the work done. The application software is going to help us to sort out all of the data that we are working on, based on the results form the user.

When all of this is done, the end-user is going to be able to take all of the insights and the information that they have been able to gather up, and then present that data and all of their findings to those who need it. Usually, this needs to be done in a format that is really easy to share, including a table or a graph, so that it is easier for those key people, the ones who really need to use the information, to see what insights are there.

Data mining is going to be a composite type of discipline and will represent a variety of methods and techniques that are used in different types of analytic capabilities. This can be useful because it is able to address a ton of the needs of your company and can ask different types of questions and use different levels of human rules or inputs in order to come to this decision. There are a few different parts that are going to come into play here when we are working with a data mining process, and these are going to include:

Descriptive modeling is the first type of data mining that we need to take a look at and use on our process. This kind of modeling is going to be responsible for uncovering some of the shared similarities or the groupings that are found in historical data. This is going to help us to determine the reasons behind the success or failure of a company. For example, it can help us to categorize out our customers by their preferences that they have to the products we sell or some of their sentiment overall. Some of the techniques that are going to fit in when we talk about descriptive modeling will include:

1. Clustering: This is when we are able to group some of the records that are similar to one another.
2. Anomaly detection: This is when we are going to work to identify some of the outliers, and then will determine whether these are important and should be looked at a bit more closely or not.
3. Association rule learning: This is when we are going to take some of the records that we have and detect whether there are some kinds of relationships between them and what those relationships are.

4. Principal component analysis: This is where we are going to take a look to detect what kind of relationship is going to be present with the variables that we are working on.
5. Affinity grouping: This is when we group people together who have a common interest or simple goals at the same time.

The second thing that we are going to take a look at is predictive modeling. This modeling is going to go deeper to classify events in the future, or to help you to estimate outcomes that are not known. An example of how this one work could including using credit scoring to help us determine how likely it is that someone is going to repay their loan or not. The idea of predictive modeling is that it helps us to uncover some of the insights that we need on topics like customer churn, credit defaults, and campaign responses. Some of the techniques that we are able to use that work with this one will include:

1. Regression: This is going to be a measure of the strength that we see between one dependent variable and a series of variables that are independent.

2. Neural networks: This is a complicated type of computer program that can be set up in order to learn, make its own predictions, and even detect some of the patterns that are found in your own data as well.

3. Decision trees; These are going to be a type of diagram, that is shaped like a tree, that can help you to make some decisions. The point with this one is that you are able to take a look at each of the branches and see the probable occurrence of each part. This helps us to see which one is the best option for us when making a decision.

4. Support vector machine: This is going to be an example of a supervised learning model from machine learning that can help our model to learn the way that it should.

And finally, we are going to take a look at a process that is known as prescriptive modeling. Thanks to the growth that we are seeing with that unstructured data and all of the things that we are able to do with it, the prescriptive modeling is growing in popularity all of the time. Think about how many sources of unstructured data we are able to work with including audio, PDFs, email, books, comment fields, the web and any other source of text that we are able to encounter to help us to figure out the data that we need. Thanks to all of this, the adoption of text mining as a related discipline to data mining is also something that has seen a significant amount of growth.

It is important for us to have the ability to go through and successfully parse, filter, and transform unstructured data in order to include it with some of our own predictive models, in order to improve the amount of accuracy that is going to happen with our predictions.

In the end, we need to make sure that we are not looking at data mining as its own separate and standalone kind of entity because some of the other parts of data science such as pre-processing are equally as important in this process as well. Prescriptive modeling looks at internal and external variables and constraints to recommend using one or more courses of action. For example, when we are able to work with this, we may be able to use it to figure out some of the best marketing offers to send out to the different customers that we are working with overall.

Why Is It So Important?

Another question that a lot of companies and even individuals are going to have about data mining is why this process is so important? When we take a look at all of the data that is being collected, and even more at the data that is currently being created, we can start to get a closer look at why this data mining process, and some of the other steps of data science, are going to be so important to your business.

Most businesses have already been able to see some of the staggering numbers that are going to meet them. The volume of data that is being produced right now is already huge, and it is predicted that this data is going to double every two years. Unstructured data on its own, which is the main form of data that you are going to collect because it is easier and cheaper, is able to make up about 90 percent of the digital universe right now. But more information, while it may seem like a great thing, does not necessarily mean that we have more knowledge right off the bat.

We will find that with data mining, we are able to complete a number of the tasks that we would like to and see some results with all of our hard work. For example, we are going to find that with the process of data mining, we are able to:

1. Sift through all of the noise, the repetitive and the chaotic noise, that may show up in your set of data.
2. It helps you to understand what is relevant and important while ignoring that noise from before, and then make good use out of that information

in order to assess the outcomes that are the most likely.

3. It can accelerate the pace of making decisions. Plus, the decisions are going to be backed by data, rather than just a guess or your intuition, so you know they are sound and good ones to work with.

All of these reasons and more are why many businesses are interested in working with the raw data that they spend time collecting and using things like data mining to help them get through that data. Only with data mining and the right machine learning and Python tools are we able to really find the hidden patterns and relationships in all of that data, and then use those to make better decisions and improve our business.

There are a lot of people and companies who are willing to work with the data mining process as well. You will be able to find this kind of process in almost any field that gathers up and relies on the data that they collect over time. And as more industries and companies learn about data science, data analysis, and machine learning, it is likely that more people will choose to add this to the process as well. Some examples of the industries who are able to work with data science to improve the way that they do business will include:

1. Communications: Many telecommunication and multimedia companies are going to use some of the analytic models that come with this to help them make sense of all the customer data that they have. This ensures that they are able to make some targeted campaigns that actually work for them.

2. Education: This can help teachers and other educators come up with a great and individualized plan for those students who may need a little extra help with learning or grasping some of the information that they should.

3. Banking: All financial institutions would be able to benefit from using this data science process. It is great for recommending what kinds of products should be offered to customers over time, can make sure that there isn't any fraud or money laundering going on in the company, and can help to determine who should be eligible for a loan or not.

4. Insurance; With analytic help, these insurance companies will find that it is a lot easier for them to solve big problems with risk management, customer attrition, compliance, and fraud to name a few issues. Companies have been able to use the techniques that come with data mining in order to find new ways to offer products that are competitive to their customer base right now to keep those customers around.

5. Manufacturing: Making sure that the supply plans and the demand forecasts are aligned is going to be critical. And these companies need to make sure that they can quickly detect problems, work on quality assurance, and investment in the equity of the brand. These companies are able to use data science in order

to help them out with anticipating maintenance, saving time and money in the process.
6. Retail: These retail companies are able to gather up a ton of information on their customers through the purchases that the customer is able to make in the store or online. The retail company can use this to help out with some of the marketing campaigns that these companies are going to work with, helps them to figure out which products they would like to offer next, and so much more.

There are so many industries that are going to benefit when it comes to working with data science, and as time goes on, it is likely that more and more of these companies are going to jump on board. It is easy to see how data science, and data mining, are going to benefit these companies, and it is a no-brainer to figure out just why they would want to learn more about it and use it for their own needs as well.

Data Warehousing and Mining Software

Data mining programs are abundantly used by many companies, and they are going to be there to help us analyze the relationships and patterns that are found in all of that data, usually being based on the request of the user. For example, a company is able to use this data mining software to help them to create some classes of information that they would like to use.

To help us to illustrate this point, let's imagine that there is a restaurant that we want to follow, one who is interested in using some of the processes that come with data mining in order to make it easier to offer the right specials at the right time. They want to make sure that these specials will hit the right customers and make them the most money possible in the process. This company is going to take a look at all of the information that it has been able to collect and then will create some classes, based on when a customer came to eat, and what they ended up ordering.

Of course, this is just one example of how we are able to use the process of data mining to improve our business. In some other situations, a data miner is able to find a cluster of information based on a logical relationship, or they will look at the associations and sequential patterns in order to draw up a few conclusions about trends that are seen in consumer behavior.

During this time, we have to remember the importance that comes with warehousing in data mining. Warehousing is a simple process where companies are going to pick out one program or database in order to centralize all of the raw data that they are working with. With a data warehouse, the company is able to spin off the needed segments of the data over to specific users so that it can be analyzed and ready to go when needed.

However, it is possible in some cases where the analyst is going to start off with the kind of data that they want to use and then they are able to create a data warehouse based on those specs in the first place. Regardless of hose a business and some other entities are going to store and organize their data, they will want to make sure that it is used in a manner that will support the decisions that the management of that entity is going to make.

There is so much that we are going to be able to do when it comes to the process of data mining. This is the part of the data science project that we are going to focus on more because it helps us to really know what to do with the data at hand and makes it easier to finish some of the data analysis that we need to do. When we are done working with the data mining process, we will have a better understanding of what information is inside of our data, and how we can use that information for our own needs.

Chapter 7: Some of the Basics of Data Mining with Python

In the previous chapter, we spent a bit of time taking a look at the basics of data mining and what we are able to do with this method. Now we need to take a look at some of the specifics that come with this process, and how we are able to use it along with the Python coding language that we discussed above as well. Let's take a look at some of the different ways that we can work with Python and the data mining process together.

Creating a Regression Model in Python

One of the best ways that we can ensure that we learn how to work with data mining and Python is to actually put these to work and see how they go. We want to start off with creating a good estimate of the linear relationship that will show up between variables, print off the coefficients of the correlation, and then will be able to plot a line of best fit at the same time. To help us out, we are going to use the House Sales data set that can be found here: https://www.kaggle.com/harlfoxem/housesalesprediction/kernels.

This data is going to have information that we need on the prices of the homes and the characteristics of these homes as well, so our goal is to see whether or not we are able to make a model that can estimate the relationship that happens between the price of the house, and how many square feet that house has to start with.

The first step here to make sure that things work how we want is to install Jupyter on your desktop. This is going to be a free platform that we can use as a processor for the IPython notebooks that we will be using, and because of the intuition that comes with it, we are going to enjoy using this as a beginner's tool. You will also notice that we will focus on the Pandas library to help us get started as well.

So, the first part of the code that we need to focus on is going to be below. Add this to your compiler and then we will take a moment to talk about some of it to see how data mining works in particular:

In [1]:

```
import pandas as pd
import matplotlib.pyplot as plt
import numpy as np
import scipy.stats as stats
import seaborn as sns
from matplotlib import rcParams

%matplotlib inline
%pylab inline
```

Populating the interactive namespace from numpy and matplotlib

Now to start with, the code above took some time to add in the different data science libraries that we need to use in order to get started on our project. We installed NumPy, Matplotlib, and SciPy because these are some of the extensions and the features that we will need to make this work. You must make sure that these are installed on your system before starting to ensure that you are able to use them the way that you want.

We are now going to break down the code that we imported above into a few steps so that we can figure out how we can apply data mining in order to solve a regression problem, doing it one step at a time. in real life, it is likely that you are not going to have someone hand you a set of data to work with and the right machine learning techniques so remember that you will need to go through and gather the data before cleaning and organizing it for your needs. But to help us learn some of the basics of how to work with this code, and to ensure that we are able to get started, we are going to work with this to keep things easier. Let's take a look at the next part of the code that we need to use in order to get started with this process as well:

In [2]:

; id; date; price; bedrooms; bathrooms; sqft_living; sqft_lot
0; 7129300520; 20141013T000000; 221900.0; 3; 1.00; 1180; 5650
1; 6414100192; 20141209T000000; 538000.0; 3; 2.25; 2570; 7242
2; 5631500400; 20150225T000000; 180000.0; 2; 1.00; 770; 10000
3; 2487200875; 20141209T000000; 604000.0; 4; 3.00; 1960; 5000
4; 1954400510; 20150218T000000; 510000.0; 3; 2.00; 1680; 8080

```
df =
pd.read_csv('/Users/michaelrundell/Desktop/kc_house
_data.csv')
df.head()
Out[2]:
```
Reading the csv file from Kaggle using pandas (pd.read_csv).

In [3]:
```
df.isnull().any()
Out[3]:
```

```
id              False
date              False
price           False
bedrooms          False
bathrooms         False
sqft_living     False
sqft_lot        False
...
dtype: bool
```

Checking to see if any of our data has null values. If there were any, we'd drop or filter the null values out.

In [4]:

df.dtypes

Out[4]:

```
id              int64
date              object
price           float64
bedrooms          int64
bathrooms         float64
sqft_living       int64
sqft_lot          int64
...
dtype: object
```

Ok, at first this is going to seem like a mess and it is hard to understand what is here to start with. But now we are going to spend some time going through all of this to figure out what is there, and why all of it is going to be so important to the work that we are trying to accomplish.

To start here, we took some time to import the data frame from the CSV file with the help of the Pandas library. Then we made sure to check whether or not this would read in the proper manner. The isnull() function is in place to make sure that any of the data we have will be usable for the regression that we want to accomplish.

When we are doing this in real life, a single column could possibly have the data in the form of strings, integers, or NaN, all in one place. This means that you will need to take some time in your own project to double-check that all of the types are matching and that the data you are using is going to be suitable for the regression that you are doing here. Since we are just doing a practice one here, the set of data that we are using is going to be prepared already, so it is ready to go, unlike most other databases.

With this in mind, it is time for us to get a better understanding of the data that we are working with before we go any further. It is important for us to go through the shape of the data and see whether or not the data seems to be reasonable or not. Corrupted data is not that uncommon so it is going to be good practice for us to run two checks, otherwise, the information that we get in our algorithm is not going to be as accurate as we would like.

In the first check, we are going to use the function of df.describe(). This one is helpful to work with because it helps us to look at all of the variables that are found in our analysis. When that part is done, we are going to spend some time plotting the histograms of the variables that the analysis is targeting using the function of plt.pyplot.hist(). The coding that we are going to work with here, and the output that comes with it will include:

In [5]:
df.describe()
Out[5]:

	price	bedrooms	bathrooms	sqft_living
count	21613	21613	21613	21613
mean	540088.10	3.37	2.11	2079.90
std	367127.20	0.93	0.77	918.44
min	75000.00	0.00	0.00	290.00
25%	321950.00	3.00	1.75	1427.00
50%	450000.00	3.00	2.25	1910.00
75%	645000.00	4.00	2.50	2550.00
max	7700000.00	33.00	8.00	13540.00

Quick takeaways: We are working with a data set that contains 21,613 observations, the mean price is approximately $540k, the median price is approximately $450k, and the average house's area is 2080 ft2

```
fig = plt.figure(figsize=(12, 6))
sqft = fig.add_subplot(121)
cost = fig.add_subplot(122)

sqft.hist(df.sqft_living, bins=80)
sqft.set_xlabel('Ft^2')
sqft.set_title("Histogram of House Square Footage")
```

```
cost.hist(df.price, bins=80)
cost.set_xlabel('Price ($)')
cost.set_title("Histogram of Housing Prices")

plt.show()
```

In the coding that we did above, we used matplotlib to help us print out two different histograms. Go ahead and work through this one to see how these histograms are going to look through in your compiler. These are going to show us the distribution of housing prices compared to the square footage that is in each house.

What we are going to find here is that both variables are going to come with a distribution that is skewed to the right, though one is a bit more than the other. This is going to provide us with a good sense of the set of data that we are working with, and we also know more about the distributions of the variables that we would like to measure as well.

With all of this in place, we are able to move on and work with our regression analysis to learn more about the information and how it is able to help us. First, we will need to import the stats models to get the least-squares regression estimator function. The module that we are going to use here is known as the Ordinary Least Squares, and it is going to take on the majority of the work when it comes to crunching some of the numbers that we need for a Python regression. The coding that we are going to need to make this one happens will include the following:

In [15]:

```
import statsmodels.api as sm
from statsmodels.formula.API import ols
```

When you code to produce a linear regression summary with OLS with only two variables this will be the formula that you use:

Reg = ols('Dependent variable ~ independent variable(s), dataframe).fit()

print(Reg.summary())

When we look at housing prices and square footage for houses in King's county, we print out the following summary report:

In [16]:

```
m = ols('price ~ sqft_living',df).fit()
print (m.summary())
```

When we take a few moments to print out the summary that we need for this regression, all of the information that is relevant to our questions will be easily found. This is going to include things like the coefficients of correlation, standard error, t-statistics, R-squared, and more. Looking at what output we are able to get form this, it is clear that there is going to be a huge relationship that shows up in the market between the housing prices and the square footage of the house.

When you go through this, you will find that there is also a decent amount of magnitude that shows up in the process as well. For example, every time we add in additional 100-square feet to home, we will find that the pricing of that house, on average, is going to be about $28,000 higher. It is easy to adjust this formula in order to include more than one variable that is independent, based on what information we would like to be able to do with this kind of program.

As we can see, working with a regression problem in Python and using it to help us sort through some of our data and learn more about how this process is meant to work is going to be beneficial to us in many ways. In the examples above, we spent our time looking at what correlation between the housing prices and the amount of square footage that was in the house for a specific market. But we can work with the same kind of idea no matter what our business problem may be, or how we would like to work with this data science process.

Chapter 8: Your Complete Course to Working with the Pandas Library

One of the best libraries that you can depend on when it comes to handling data science, especially when you are relying on the Python language to help you out, is the Pandas library. This is going to be a fantastic library to work with for data science because it is able to handle each and every part. It can take you through all of the life cycles of data science that we talked about before, making it much easier for you to handle your data, get it organized and ready to go and to ensure that you will be able to take on the analysis and the visualizations as they are needed.

To help us to get started, we need to take a few minutes to learn more about the Pandas library and what it all entails. Pandas are considered an open-sourced package from Python that is going to provide us with many of the tools that are needed to complete any data analysis that we would like. This package also comes with a few different types of data structures that we can learn about and then use for many of the different tasks of manipulating data as needed. For someone who is wanting to sort through data and get it all done in a quick and orderly fashion while learning the insights and the predictions that are in that data, this is the best library for you.

In addition to many of the tasks that we have taken some time to learn about above, the Pandas library is also going to provide us with many methods that programmers can use when they want to handle their own data analysis. This is always a good thing in the process of data science, and Pandas is sure to be the library that you run to when you have a big project in data science, and you want to make sure that it is done right.

While we are here and talking about the Pandas library, it is important that we stop and take a look at some of the advantages that programmers are going to notice when they decide to use this library over some of the others. This library is definitely one of the best options to consider learning and have around for almost any of the data science projects that you would like to focus on, so at least learning how it works, and some of the coding that is necessary to ensure that it behaves the way that it should it be going to be really helpful with your own projects. Some of the various advantages that data scientists are going to be able to enjoy when working with Pandas includes:

1. It is going to take the data that you have and present it in a manner that is suitable for analyzing the large amounts of data that you have. This data analysis is going to be completed in Pandas with the use of the DataFrame and the Series data structures.
2. You will find that the Pandas package is going to come with many methods to help us filter through our data in a convenient manner while seeing some great results.

3. Pandas also come with a variety of utilities that are going to help us when it is time to perform the input and output operations in a manner that is quick and seamless. In addition, Pandas is able to read data that comes in a variety of formats, which is very important in data science, such as Excel, TSV, and CSV to name a few.

You will find that Pandas is really going to change up the game and how you do some coding when it comes to analyzing the data a company has with Python. In fact, it is often the most used, and the most preferred tool in data wrangling and munging (we will look at how to do this more in the next chapter) in the Python language and elsewhere as well. Pandas are going to be free to use and open source and were meant to be used by anyone who is looking to handle the data they have in a safe, fast, and effective manner.

As we mentioned above, there are actually quite a few Python libraries out there that we are able to use, and some of them are going to be great for data science as well. But there are many data scientists, and the companies they work for, who like to rely on Pandas because of the many benefits, the fact that it can handle all of your projects, and all of the neat features.

One thing that you may find as really cool about this library is that it is able to take some of your data, whether this data comes from a database, a CSV or TSV file, and then it can take the information that we are able to find in that file and turn it into an object in Python. This is going to be changed a bit over the different rows and columns and we are going to refer back to it as a data frame. But it is going to look pretty similar to what we are used to seeing with an Excel kind of table.

Now, if this is not the first time that you have done any coding before, especially if you have worked with the R programming language before, then the objects that you create here are going to share some similarities to what we see with R as well. And these objects are going to make it so much easier for us to do our work, especially when we want to get it all done without any list comprehension or dictionaries in the process.

Loops are an important part of the Python code that we are not going to have a lot of time to discuss and look over in this guidebook, but they help us to get the compiler to read through the same part of the code. These are great, but sometimes with our data analysis the loops are going to be a bit chunky and will take up more space than we would like. And sometimes they are just too much to handle. Working with the idea of objects in the code and how these can handle the Python parts that we would like can help us to get the same thing done in the coding without quite as much mess.

For the most part here though, you will find that it is often best if you take the time to download the Pandas library, and you should do this at the same time that you download your Python library especially if your main goal is to go through and work on a data science project in the end. If you already have the Python language ready to go on your computer though, and then later decide to work with data science and the Pandas library, then this is still a pretty easy process to work with for many programmers.

The best way to download the Pandas library for this method is to go to the www.pandas.org website and then look for the version that goes with your operating system. It will only take a few minutes to download the Pandas library, and then you will be able to use all of the functionality that comes with it as well here.

Once you have taken the time to get the Pandas library downloaded on your computer, it is time to learn a bit more about some of the steps and the process involved in getting this to work. You will find that once we get into this library and learn some of the basics of coding with it, it can be a fun language with all of the features and capabilities that come with it. Plus, when you learn how to use this kind of language, it is going to make it easier to complete the data analysis that you would like.

At this point, we have the Pandas library downloaded and ready to use, and now it is time to focus on what kind of steps need to happen in order to load up the data that we want, and even save that data, before we try to use Pandas to run the data through those algorithms we plan to make. when it is time to work with Pandas to take that data that you have collected and learned from it, we have to remember that there are going to be three main methods that Pandas allows us to use to get all of this done. These three methods are pretty simple to work with, and will include:

1. You can convert a NumPy array, a Python list or a Python dictionary over to the data frame that is available with Pandas.
2. You can open up a local file that is found on your computer with the help of Pandas. This is often going to be something like a CSV file, but it is possible that it could be something else like Excel or a delimited text file in some cases.
3. You can also choose to use this in order to open up a file or another database that is remote, including a JSON or CSV that is located on a website through a URL or you can have the program read through it on a database or a table that is from SQL.

Now, as you go through with these three steps, we have to remember that there are actually a couple of commands that will show up for each one, and it depends on which method you go with what command you will choose. However, one thing that all three shares in common are that the command they use to open up a data file will be the same. The command that you need to use to open up your data file, regardless of the method above that you choose to use will include:

Pd.red_filetype()

During this time, you will find that when it is time to work with this Pandas library, there is going to be a large variety of arguments that you are able to choose from. Of course, taking the time here to learn what all of them mean and how you should pull them up at which times is a challenge and would take too long for us to complete. To help move things along and not make it overwhelming in the process, we are going to make sure that we are just focusing our attention on the arguments that are necessary for this project, and the ones that are needed for completing a good data analysis in the process. We will leave the rest alone for now and you can learn them as they are needed for any individual projects that you need later.

With all of this in mind and ready to go, it is time for us to learn more about how we are able to convert one of the objects that we already have in use in Python, whether this is a list or a dictionary for example, over to the Pandas library. This is necessary to make sure that the object is usable for our project. The simple command that we will need to use to make this conversion happen and go as smoothly as possible includes:

Pd.DataFrame()

With the code above, the part that goes inside of the parenthesis is where we are able to specify the different object, and sometimes the different objects, that are being created inside that data frame. This is the command that will bring out a few arguments, and you can choose which ones of those you want to work with here as well.

When we do end up at this point, it should be easy to see that the data we need is already loaded up, so now we need to move on to the next part and look at some of the different parts of inspecting that we are able to do here as well. To get this started we need to first take a look at the frame of the data, and then get a better look at whether or not this is going to match up with some of the parts that we want or expect it to.

To make sure that we can get this done, and to make sure we can do this, we need to run the name of the data frame that we would like to choose to help us bring up the entire table. We are also able to take this a bit further and limit things to add in the control that we would like. Sometimes, we do not want to work with the whole table, just a small part of it, and this is something that we can do as well.

For example, if we would like to go through this process and only get a certain number of rows in the beginning, you can decide how many of these rows are necessary to get the work done, you would be able to use the function of fdf.heat(n) to get it done. Or if your goal is to work with a certain number of rows that are at the end of your table, the function that you would need to make this happen is df.tail(n).

The df.shape option is going to help if we are working with the number of rows and columns that show up, and if you would like the option to gather up some of the information that is already present in the data type, the index, or the memory, the only code that is needed to complete this part is df.info().

This is just the start of some of the codes that you are able to do with the Pandas library to help make sure that things get done. For example, you are able to use the command s.value_counts(dropna=False) and find that it allows you to take a look at the unique counts and values that are in the series, such as you would use if you just want to work with one, up to a few, columns, at a time.

Another command that you may find useful to work with here is going to be the function df.describe(). This one is going to be a helpful one to work with because it allows you to input some of your summary statistics, the ones that come with the numerical columns in your graph. You can also use a variety of codes and functions to help you to get all of the statistics that are needed from an entire series or an entire data frame.

Now, this may seem like a lot of information to spend our time on right now, but to ensure that we are able to make full sense of the things that we are doing right here, and what all of the parts mean, it is important to take a look at some of the most common commands that we are going to see in Pandas that can help with data science. Some of the most common commands that help us to view and inspect the data that we are working with will include:

1. df.mean(). This function is going to help us get the mean of all our columns.
2. df.corr() This function is going to return the correlation between all of the columns that we have in the frame of data.

3. Df.count(): This function is going to help us return the number of non-null values in each of the frames of data based on the columns.
4. Df.max(). The function is going to return the highest value in each of the columns.
5. Df.min(). This function is going to return the lowest value that is found in each of the columns that you have.
6. Df.median(). This is going to be the function that you can use when you want to look at each column and figure out the median.
7. Df.std(). This function is going to be the one that you would use in order to look at each of the columns and then find the standard deviation that comes with it.

All of those are going to be great options that you are able to work with when you want to take that data frame that we were talking about before and put it to good use. Another neat thing that we can spend some of our time on when working on the Pandas library is to join together and even combine some of the different parts that come in our database.

This is going to be done with a basic type of command in Python, so learning how to work with it is going to be a simple thing that you are able to work with. But it is also something that is important to learn about in the beginning. But it is going to be the thing that you need to do in order to combine or join together the data or the frames. With this in mind, there are going to be three types of commands that are needed to ensure that this process happens in Pandas, and they are going to include the following:

1. Dfl.appent(df2). This one is going to add in the rows of df1 to the end of df2. You need to make sure that the columns are going to be identical in the process.
2. Df.concat([df1, df2], axis=1). This command is going to add in the columns that you have in df1 to the end of what is there with df2. You want to make sure that you have the rows added together as being identical.
3. Dfl.oin(df2, on=col1, hot='inner'). This is going to be an SQL style join the columns in the df1 with the columns on df2 where the rows for col identical values have how can be equal to one of left, right, inner, and outer.

There is so much that we are able to do when it comes to the Pandas library, and that is one of the reasons why it is such a popular option to go with. Many companies who want to work with data science are also going to be willing to add on the Pandas extension because it helps them to do a bit more with data science, and the coding is often simple thanks to the Python language that runs along with it.

The commands that we were able to take a look at during this chapter are some of the basic options that we can learn how to work with along with the Pandas library, but they are meant to help us learn a bit more about this language, and all of the neat things that the Pandas library is able to help us out with. Pandas is a great option to work with no matter what kind of data science project you are working with, and it is definitely worth your time to learn how to use this to create your Python libraries and models, and to ensure that your analytics are as good as possible.

And that is the introduction that you need to see some success with the Python coding language. You will find that this is just the start of the process and that the more you work with the Pandas library on your data analysis, the greater results you will be able to see. Without taking too long, you will soon be able to write out some strong models and codes that can help you to bring out the data that your company needs and can provide you with the insights and predictions that you need.

Chapter 9: Using Your Data to Make Smart Business Decisions

Learning how to work with data science is going to be a very important part of your business plan. Putting it all together and ensuring that you understand how the different parts are going to work, and adequately going through all of the different steps that come with data science, is going to be critical to ensuring that you get the results that you would like.

Many businesses are willing to go out and collect data on the industry, on their competition, and on their customers. But then they start to run into trouble because they are not sure what should happen next. They have all of this data readily available to use, but they have no idea how to go through and really read through that information and see what is there for them to use. It is not enough to just collect this data though; we need to be willing and able to use it for our needs as well and figuring out how to use the data science process is going to make this a little bit easier as well.

Data science is meant to help businesses to actually use the data they have been able to collect. There is just too much raw data, and it is usually in a format that is unstructured and hard to read through, for someone to manually go through and see what kind of insights are present in it. This may sound like a better idea and less complicated than some of the steps that we have discussed in this guidebook. But when you consider that there could potentially be millions of data points that we need to go through in order to find our insights and predictions, it becomes a lot easier to understand why this is impossible to do manually.

Instead of having an employee who has to manually go through all of the data to find those insights, we can choose to work with data science, and some of the algorithms that are present with Python, in order to get through that information faster and more efficiently. It still takes some time and experimenting with the different models and algorithms that we want to use, but it is going to make things a lot easier to work with overall.

The goal of this process is to take that raw data, the data that seems to be all over the place and hard to read and turn it into a method that we are able to easily work with. You will find that with the right Python algorithm and the help of machine learning, that we are able to take all of that data and actually find some hidden information and insights that are actually able to improve your business and make things better for your own bottom line in the process.

There are a lot of decisions that these algorithms and this whole process are able to help you out with. You may find that they can help you to figure out how to meet the needs of your customers a little bit better. If you use some of the survey responses and maybe even some of the comments that come with social media, you can find new ways to interact and meet the needs of your customers, maybe some that your competition hasn't been able to think about yet.

Another benefit is figuring out what products to release. With the help of data science, you can listen to your customers, try out a few basic versions of the product, and slowly design something that your customers would actually spend money on. This is something that used to carry a lot of risk in the past because it was hard to know for sure whether something was going to take off in the market or not. But with the help of data science and using that raw data to your advantage through these algorithms, you will be able to figure out the best product ahead of time to sell and have more certainty that it is the one your customers want.

Through data science, you may be able to figure out a new market to enter, one that your competition hasn't had time to get to yet. Sometimes, when we are working with our models, we will notice that most of the data points are going to follow one trend, and maybe that is the one that we are already in and using. But then we may also notice that there are a significant number of outliers on your charts as well. These outliers, if the group is large enough or enough of them are close together, will show us a new market that would be great for entering, or a new demographic to work with as well.

Sometimes these methods are going to help us figure out the best ways to reduce the amount of waste that is going on in the company. Every company has some kind of waste, whether it is a process that is not as effective as it should be, too many or too few employees working on something, downtime where things are not getting done, or something else. Some companies have been able to utilize the data science to learn more about the processes that are used in their business, and how to reduce the amount of waste. The more that we are able to reduce this waste and keep it to a minimum, the more money can be added to our bottom line, without reducing the quality of the product or the service that is being offered to the customer.

Learning how to beat out the competition is always one of the benefits that we are able to see when working with the process of data science. You will be able to use this to help you figure out new ways to reach your market, how to make different decisions that set you apart and more. You should go in with a clear objective of how you would like to reach your target audience and how you would like to beat out the competition, but the models and algorithms that we include with data science can make this a bit easier to accomplish.

In some areas like manufacturing, this data science is able to help them to work with their system and learn when machines and other parts are likely to fail. When we know that something is going to need to be fixed by a certain date, it is easier to make plans to do it during a slow time, such as at night. This prevents loss of time of work with the part breaking in the middle of a workday and then being without any work getting done for a few days as the part is ordered and put back in. All of this can be done on a good schedule that allows us to take care of the machine or the part, get it fixed when needed, and to keep production going on time.

And finally, some companies will find that using data science is a great way for them to market and advertise to their customers better than before. When you are able to learn more about your target audience and what they are looking for, it becomes a lot easier to go through the process of figuring out what kind of marketing campaigns you should work with as well. This is going to make a big difference in the results that you get, what kinds of campaigns you try to use, and more as well.

As we can see here, there are a lot of times when working with data science is going to help you to make some of the best and most informed decisions possible for your business. In the past, these decisions had to be made on guesses and the little information that you were able to gather. But there was always some kind of risk that came with these decisions. Today, we are able to use data science, the Python coding language, and machine learning to help us make these decisions and know that they are not as risky because they are backed by data and research instead.

Conclusion

Thank you for making it through to the end of *Python Data Science*, let's hope it was informative and able to provide you with all of the tools you need to achieve your goals whatever they may be.

The next step is to start learning how you are able to implement the basics of data science and Python into your own business as well. These are big buzzwords that have been flying around the world of business, no matter what industry the business is in, and many companies are ready to jump right in and see what this data science can do for them. But actually, taking some of the steps that are needed and learning how to work with the data life cycle and all of the different processes that we need with this can make a difference, and taking that first step can be hard. This guidebook has taken the time to look at all of these different parts to explore how a business can get started with data science for their own needs.

There are a lot of different parts that come with the data science life cycle, and while it may seem like more fun to just create the model and be done with it, all of these steps are going to be very important to the results that we are looking to get. We have to work through the collection of raw data, cleaning off and organizing the data that we have, learning what insights are there, figuring out the best model to work with and training and testing it, and then completing the analysis as well. We will take some time to discuss all of these parts and more as we worked through this guidebook and figure out the best way to make these works for us as well.

The data science process is going to provide you with a ton of benefits overall, and you are going to enjoy how it is going to be in order to use this information to learn more about your customers, about your competition and more, so you can increase your bottom line and see some results with your business. It may take some time, and often it may take some programming knowledge and more to get it done. But you will find that with the help of the Python coding language, and some of the machine learning that we have discussed in this guidebook, you will be able to make this work for your needs.

Working with data science is something that all businesses are able to use to help them get ahead and really see some results in the process. But it is a process that takes time and is not always as easy to complete as we might hope. With the help of this guidebook, and some of the tools that we have discussed inside, get ready to use Python data science for your needs.

Finally, if you found this book useful in any way, a review on Amazon is always appreciated!